Busy Highways

Written by Marilyn Woolley

Series Consultant: Linda Hoyt

WorldWise
Content-based Learning

Contents

Introduction

Animals on the move

Every year around the world some animals travel long distances. They make their journeys to find food, safe places to raise their young and better weather. Some of these animals fly through the air, some swim or drift through the ocean, and others walk or crawl long distances over land. Then they return to where they first began their journey. We call this migration.

Most of these migrating animals move together as part of a large group, but some travel alone. Some move within a country, and others travel across countries and oceans. Some go along one **route** and then return along another route.

The routes these animals take create busy highways.

Did you know?

All animals that migrate have special body features and behaviours that enable them to travel long distances.

Chapter 1

Air migration

Every year, millions of birds fly long distances to breed, nest and feed before returning to where they came from. They fly from cold places to places that are warmer and where there is plenty of food.

Migrating birds fly together in large flocks along a **route** called a **flyway**. They use the wind and **air currents** to help them and to save energy. They work together to keep moving in the direction they want to go.

Did you know?

Each year, millions of bird species, including the albatross, snow goose and peregrine falcon, migrate to the Arctic in summertime. They feed, make nests and raise their young.

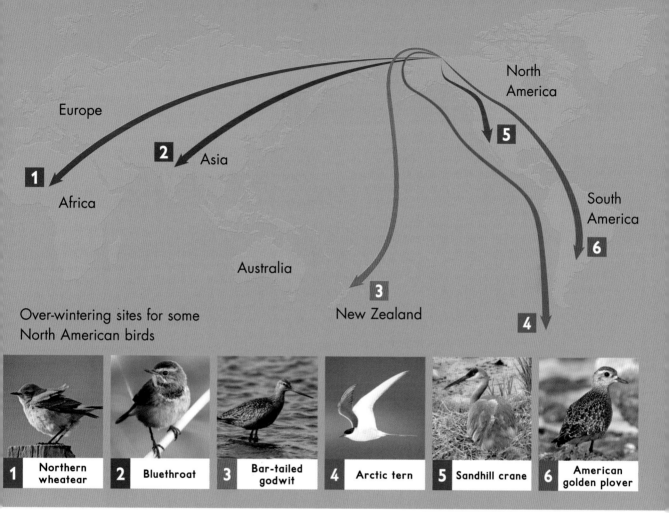

Europe

2

Asia

1

Africa

North
America

5

South
America

6

Australia

3

New Zealand

4

Over-wintering sites for some
North American birds

1 Northern
wheatear

2 Bluethroat

3 Bar-tailed
godwit

4 Arctic tern

5 Sandhill crane

6 American
golden plover

Find out more

Which bird flies
further than any
other bird?
Where does it go?
How does it get
there and back?

The bar-tailed godwit's epic flight

The bar-tailed godwit is a large wading bird. It makes one of the longest migrations in the animal world.

Flying from New Zealand

During summer in the Southern Hemisphere (November to March), bar-tailed godwits feed along the coastline of New Zealand. As the weather cools, they fly north to the Arctic region of Alaska to breed. On the way, they stop on the coastlines of the Yellow Sea in China to rest and feed on the clams, worms and insects in the mudflats. They use their long bills to **probe** down to the bottom of the mud.

When they arrive in Alaska, in the United States, they are healthy and well fed. They have flown just over 11,000 kilometres.

Did you know?

The godwit's feathers are not waterproof so it cannot land while it is flying over the ocean.

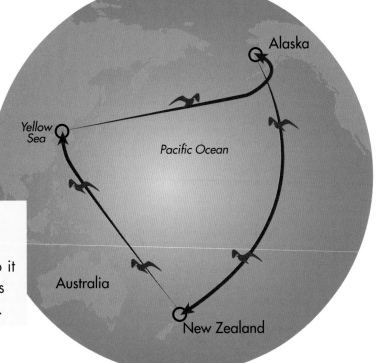

Alaska

Yellow Sea

Pacific Ocean

Australia

New Zealand

Summer in Alaska

The birds breed and raise their young during the Alaskan summer. Flocks of over 10,000 bar-tailed godwits nest on grass near pools of melting snow on the coastlines. The female lays eggs in the nest, and they hatch after about three weeks.

The birds feed on millions of insects that are found in the warm, moist conditions where the snow is melting. As they feed, their bodies change. Fifty per cent of their body becomes fat and they exercise their wings to make them bigger. They are preparing for a long-distance flight across the Pacific Ocean.

Non-stop back to New Zealand

During autumn, as the temperature drops in Alaska, the bar-tailed godwits set off on an epic journey south. They fly across the Pacific Ocean to New Zealand. The flight is an 11,000-kilometre non-stop journey that takes eight days.

9

How bar-tailed godwits travel

Scientists study bar-tailed godwits to find out how they can fly non-stop for eight days. This is what they have discovered:

- Godwits fly at different heights in the atmosphere (between about 2.8 kilometres and 4 kilometres above sea level).

- They can fly very fast (up to about 50 kilometres per hour) and use their store of fat.

- They breathe very efficiently. They can take in and **expel** large amounts of oxygen, which helps them to travel a long way without getting tired.

- As they fly, they slow down some of their organs to rest their bodies. Scientists think they might even "shut down" one side of their brain at a time to rest.

Flying in a V-formation

1. The flock works together to deal with the force of the wind. They fly in a V-**formation**. Each bird flies just behind the wing tip of the bird in front. This way, they use less energy because flying is easier.

2. A leader bird flies at the front and works the hardest against the wind. It shows the flock how to **navigate**, maintain direction, and avoid headwinds and storms.

3. When it gets tired, the leader bird moves back into the flock to rest. Another bird becomes the leader.

? Did you know?

Scientists have tried to copy the V-formation flying pattern that birds use. They have discovered that FA-18 fighter planes use 12 per cent less fuel by flying behind the wing tip rather than the tail end of another plane in the formation.

11

Chapter 2

Sea migration

Many sea animals migrate to different parts of the ocean to feed and breed. They swim or drift in seawater on their long journeys.

The humpback whale's journey

Whales make some of the longest migration journeys in the animal kingdom and the longest migration of any mammal. Humpback whales travel to cold, rough waters to feed. These waters are full of plankton and fish. The whales **gorge** themselves – eating up to three tonnes of food every day. This way they build up layers of fat on their bodies.

How humpback whales catch their food

1. Groups of 15 or more whales make a circle around the fish or krill to herd them into a tight ball.

2. They blow bubbles to confuse their **prey** and slap their long fins against the water to stun them. Each whale then lunges with its mouth wide open and takes in hundreds or thousands of prey in just one gulp.

3. They push the water back out of their mouth with their tongue.

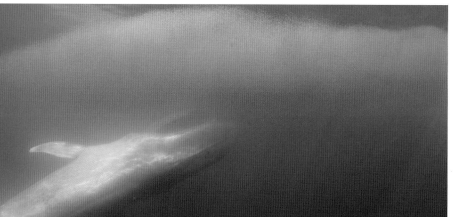

Did you know?

Humpbacks are part of a group of baleen whales that have mouth plates with bristles instead of teeth.

Find out more

How long do whale calves feed on milk from their mothers?

Spring to autumn

The cold waters around Antarctica are filled with krill – the tiny microscopic animals that humpback whales eat. Each year from September to November, hundreds of humpbacks in Australian and New Zealand waters migrate south towards the Southern Ocean. They will spend the summer feeding on krill in Antarctic waters.

The whales travel in groups called pods. They have travelled from calving areas in the warm waters along the Australian and New Zealand coasts.

Groups of young males lead the migration, while pregnant cows and cow-calf pairs follow behind.

Winter

At the start of winter in Antarctica, it becomes too cold for the humpback whales. They then return north to the warmer waters along the Australian and New Zealand coasts. This is the same area where the adult whales themselves were born. The humpbacks breed, and the females give birth to only one calf.

The humpbacks don't eat during this time. Instead, they use up the layers of fat that they gained while feeding in the cool waters off Antarctica. The females feed their calves on milk. Their calves grow quickly, and when they are about five months old and the adult whales are hungry, they return south to cooler waters to feed.

During their annual migration, they travel up to 10,000 kilometres.

Did you know?

Female humpback whales produce about 500 litres of fatty milk each day, when they are feeding their calves.

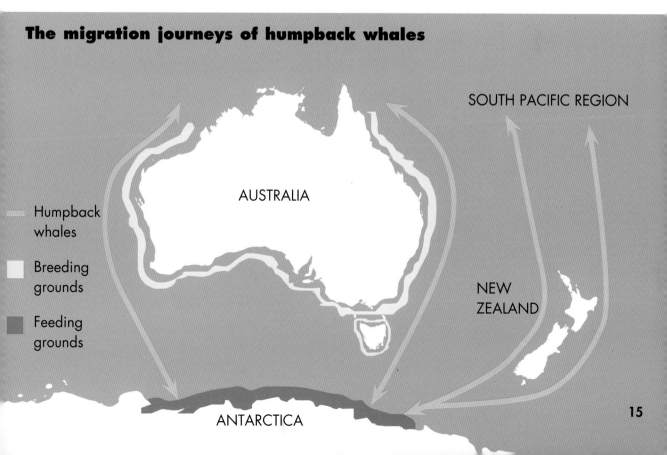

The migration journeys of humpback whales

SOUTH PACIFIC REGION

AUSTRALIA

— Humpback whales

Breeding grounds

Feeding grounds

NEW ZEALAND

ANTARCTICA

How humpback whales travel

Humpback whales are huge animals. They can grow up to 15 metres and can weigh up to 40 tonnes. They can travel at about eight kilometres an hour, but they usually swim at one to three kilometres an hour.

On their migration journey, different groups travel together – **juveniles** in one group, males in another group and females with calves in another. Within these groups humpbacks travel in small numbers of two or three, and mainly stay close to the shoreline.

The humpback has a massive tail fin, also called a fluke. It also has a long fin on each side of its body called a pectoral fin. It uses its fluke and pectoral fins to swim, turn and **propel** itself through the water.

There are two blowholes on top of its head that allow it to breathe. As the whale reaches the surface of the water, it pushes stale air through its blowholes and into the air – just like people do when using a snorkel in the water.

Find out more

Do all whales have two blowholes?

How scientists collect data

Scientists collect information about whales in different ways.

Counting: Scientists fly over the whale pods in planes and use satellites placed about 650 kilometres above Earth.

Radio tags: Scientists count whales from the air and from space. How? They attach radio tags to the whales' thick blubber. These tags transmit signals that can tell scientists the number of whales travelling together, where they are going and what they are eating.

Darts: Darts gather skin and blubber samples from the whales. These samples can help identify the tail fluke markings and what the whale has been eating.

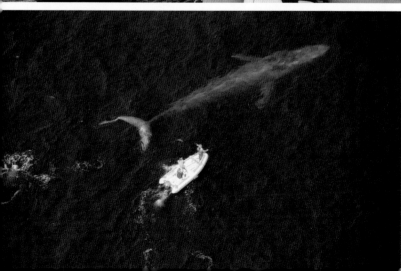

Find out more
How did the humpback whale get this name?

Chapter 3

Land migration

Mammals that migrate over land are mainly plant eaters. They travel to find new spring grasses and plants to eat. These plants give them the energy they need to keep moving.

The females need to eat plenty of food so they can produce milk for their young. Their young feed on milk until they are ready to start eating plants themselves.

The pronghorn antelope's overland passage

Pronghorn antelopes are land mammals that are found only in North America. Every year they migrate south to find food. In autumn, they leave the snow in Yellowstone National Park in Wyoming, in the United States, and travel 240 kilometres south to the warmer weather of Wyoming's Green River valley.

Summer in Yellowstone National Park

Summer in Yellowstone National Park is warm and there is plenty of food and water for the animals that live there. The pronghorn herds feed on rich grasses, sagebrush and **forbs**. In late summer, the female pronghorns give birth. They raise their young here until the end of autumn, when they travel south.

19

Winter in Green River valley

At the end of autumn in Yellowstone, it starts to snow and the **vegetation** is covered. Unlike deer, elk or moose, pronghorns cannot find their food in deep snow. A herd of about 400 pronghorn leave the park to escape the harsh winter snowfalls.

Over three days, they walk south along a river valley pathway to Wyoming's Green River valley. They eat the many plants that are growing here and stay to feed over winter until spring.

Walking back to Yellowstone

When the weather gets warmer, the snow melts and the pronghorns can begin their return journey to Yellowstone National Park. Once again they will feed and raise their young here over summer.

Did you know?

Pronghorns get plenty of moisture from the plants they eat and seldom need to drink freshwater.

How pronghorns travel

Pronghorns make a round trip of about 480 kilometres. This is one of the longest mammal migrations in North America. The migration can be **gruelling** and some animals die. Sometimes, fences, buildings and roads stop them from using their traditional migration paths and finding enough food.

The future for pronghorns in Yellowstone

The number of pronghorn in Yellowstone has declined because of **predators**, disease and extreme weather. Scientists work hard to protect the pronghorn. Laws have been changed to control the numbers that are hunted, and large areas of land have been set aside as breeding and feeding grounds.

Protecting the pronghorn

Scientists:

- place radio trackers on individual animals to check how many young survive the round trip
- follow the pronghorns and document what they see
- fit collars on the pronghorns that send signals to satellites to track their travels
- record how people are changing the migration pathway by farming it or building near or across it.

Conclusion

The journey animals make each year to breeding, nesting and feeding grounds is essential for their survival.

Scientists continue to study migrating animals to find out more about them, where they go, if they stop on the way and how they feed as they travel. Their work will help protect these animals and hopefully ensure their survival.

Glossary

air currents continuous movement of air in the same direction

expel to push something out

flyway route regularly used by migrating birds

forbs herbs other than grass

formation an orderly arrangement

gorge to eat large amounts of food

gruelling something that is very difficult

juveniles young birds or animals

navigate to find a way to get to a place

predators animals that kill and eat other animals

prey an animal that is hunted by another animal for food

probe to reach into something

propel to push or move forward

route a way to get from one place to another

thriving to successfully grow or develop

vegetation plants

Index